Rain & Sh

Sara Lynn & Diane James

Illustrations by Joe Wright

2	Falling Leaves
4	The Seasons
6	Spring
8	Coloured Eggs
10	Summer
12	Growing Cress
14	Autumn
16	Leaf Prints
18	Winter
20	Feed the Birds
22	Quiz
24	Index

TWO-CAN

What is your favourite time of year? Is it when the sun is shining brightly? Or when the rain is making puddles on the ground? Perhaps you like it best when everything is covered with thick, white snow, or the leaves are changing colour and falling off the trees.

Our year has four seasons. They are called spring, summer, autumn and winter. The weather changes from season to season.

In some parts of the world it is hot all the year round.
In other parts, it stays cold for the whole year.

The Seasons

Spring is an exciting time of the year. The weather starts to get warmer but there are often rain showers. Some plants poke up through the ground and there are lots of baby animals in the fields.

In summer, flowers start to bloom. The weather is often hot and sunny. The days seem longer because it gets dark late in the evening.

Autumn colours are beautiful. The green leaves on the trees change colour and the weather becomes cooler. There are often blustery winds. Some animals, like squirrels, start storing food. Many birds fly away to hotter countries.

In winter, it gets dark early in the evening. There are hardly any flowers in bloom and many trees lose all their leaves. The weather gets much colder and it sometimes snows. Some animals curl up and sleep until the weather gets warmer in spring.

Spring

Ducklings start hatching in spring. They chip their way out of the eggs with their beaks. Baby ducks learn to swim and fly very quickly.

Spring is the time for festivals. Many people celebrate the Easter festival by giving each other chocolate eggs.

Animals that have been sleeping all winter wake up when the weather gets warmer.

Leaves start to appear on branches that have been bare all winter. And flowers, like tulips and daffodils, push up through the warm soil.

Coloured Eggs

These coloured eggs are not chocolate, but they are good enough to eat! You could decorate some eggs for Easter presents. Keep your patterns simple and decorate eggs to give to all your friends.

Get ready...
Eggs
Wax crayon
Food colouring

Get set, go!

1 Make a pattern on an egg using a wax crayon.

2 Put the egg in a saucepan with some water and add some food colouring.

3 Ask a grown-up to boil the water and simmer for about 10 minutes.

4 When the water is cool carefully lift the egg out.

Summer

Summer is the time for going on holiday. If you go to the seaside, look out for sea creatures, such as crabs. Collect some seashells, but make sure that there are no creatures living in them!

sunflower

Birds spend a lot of time looking for food to feed their babies. What sort of food do you think they like best?

Bees and butterflies are busy visiting flowers. Which flowers do they like best?

Flowers need water as well as sunlight to help them grow. What happens when it is hot and sunny and there is no rain for days and days?

Growing Cress

Cress is one of the easiest seeds to grow. You don't need a garden because you can grow it indoors or outdoors. Cress will grow quickly and it is good to eat!

Get ready…
Packet of cress seeds
Cotton wool and a tray
Pastry cutters

Get set, go!
1 Put a pastry cutter on to a tray and push some cotton wool into the bottom.
2 Water the cotton wool to make it moist and sprinkle a thin layer of cress seeds on top.

3 After about two days your cress will probably look like the cress in the star below. After three or four days it will be ready to eat! If the cotton wool looks dry, pour some water on to the tray.

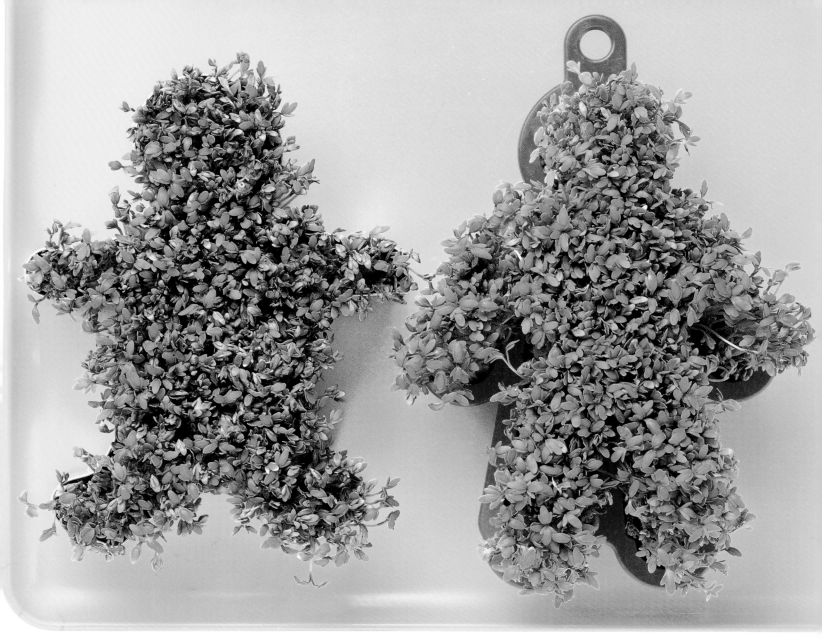

If you don't have pastry cutters, you can grow your cress in jam jar lids or a small saucer.

We made a summer salad with our cress, but you could also use it to make a delicious sandwich. Ask a grown-up to snip the cress at the top with a pair of scissors.

What other plants do people grow to eat? Which vegetables and fruit do you like best?

Autumn

In autumn, birds gather together to start their long journeys in search of warmer weather. Can you think of any birds that don't seem to mind the cold winter weather?

The leaves on many trees change from green to red, brown and gold.

Some animals eat more than usual in autumn. They also store food for the long winter months ahead when they will spend most of the time asleep. What sort of things do you think they eat?

cone

Farmers gather in the crops that have been growing all year. This is called harvest time. Some people have festivals to celebrate. Autumn is the time for apple picking.

nuts

holly

berries

Leaf Prints

Autumn is the best time of year to collect leaves because they are falling off the trees. Look for leaves that are not damaged or too dry. You can make a collection by pressing the leaves under something heavy and flat, like a large book. Or, you can make some brightly coloured leaf prints.

Get ready...
Collection of leaves
Paint and a small sponge
Newspaper and coloured paper
A flat surface

Get set, go!
1 Dab the sponge in some fairly thick paint. Use the sponge to cover one side of the leaf.
2 Place the leaf paint side down on a sheet of paper. Put a sheet of newspaper on top of the leaf and press down firmly.
3 Lift the leaf off the paper and you will have a perfect print.

How many different shapes of leaves can you find? Do you know the names of the trees that your leaves came from?

Winter

Animals that sleep through most of the winter sometimes wake up and have a snack from the food they have stored. The dormouse in the picture opposite has curled up in a ball to keep warm!

Some flowers, such as snowdrops and bluebells, poke up through the soil even when there is snow on the ground.

If the weather gets very cold, the water on ponds and lakes sometimes freezes. There may also be heavy snowfalls. Look at the next page to see how you can help birds find food, and don't forget that they may need water, too!

Feed the Birds

Many birds fly to hot countries to spend the winter. The ones that stay behind need help to find food. The ground is often too hard for them to dig for worms and insects, and there are not many plants for them to eat.

Get ready...
Selection of nuts (not salted)
Monkey nuts
Raisins
String
Strong card cup
2 short sticks

raisins

nuts

bird seed

Get set, go!

1 Take a long length of string and tie monkey nuts on to it.

2 Cut small, round holes in the side of a paper cup. Poke short sticks through the holes to act as perches. Tie a long piece of string to each end of the top stick to hang the cup up with. Fill the cup with nuts and raisins.

3 Ask a grown-up to hang up the monkey nuts and the bird feeder.

Make sure that any food you leave
for birds is out of the reach of
squirrels and cats. And don't forget
that birds need fresh water.

Quiz

When do ducklings start hatching?

Which flowers start to push up through the ground in spring?

Why do you sometimes need to water plants in the summer when it is hot and sunny?

Do you know what this huge flower is called?

What should you do to help the birds during the cold winter months?

What happens to the leaves on trees in autumn?

Index

autumn   4, 14, 16, 22
birds   4, 10, 14, 18, 22
ducks   6
Easter   6, 8
flowers   4, 6, 10, 18, 22
leaves   4, 6, 14, 16, 22
plants   4, 22
rain   22
snow   4, 18
spring   4, 6
summer   4, 10, 22
sun   22
trees   4, 14, 16, 22
winter   4, 18, 22

Photo credits
p. 2-3 © Fiona Pragoff; p. 7 Zefa; p. 8-9, 14-15, 20-21, 23 Toby;
p. 10-11, John Butcher; p. 12-13, 16-17 Graham Hitchcock;
p. 19 NHPA

First published in Great Britain in 1992 by
Two-Can Publishing Ltd
346 Old Street
London EC1V 9NQ
in association with Scholastic Publications Ltd

Copyright © Two-Can Publishing Ltd, 1992

Printed and bound in Hong Kong

2 4 6 8 10 9 7 5 3 1

British Library Cataloguing in Publication Data
James, Diane
Rain and shine. – (Jump! starts play and discover)
I. Title   III. Series.
551.607

Pbk ISBN: 1-85434-112-X
Hbk ISBN: 1-85434-164-2